POEMS OF *Love,*

From My Heart to Yours,
VOL 1

KERRY C. IRONS

outskirts press

Poems Of Love, From My Heart To Yours, Vol 1
All Rights Reserved.
Copyright © 2018 Kerry C. Irons
v5.0

The opinions expressed in this manuscript are solely the opinions of the author and do not represent the opinions or thoughts of the publisher. The author has represented and warranted full ownership and/or legal right to publish all the materials in this book.

This book may not be reproduced, transmitted, or stored in whole or in part by any means, including graphic, electronic, or mechanical without the express written consent of the publisher except in the case of brief quotations embodied in critical articles and reviews.

Outskirts Press, Inc.
http://www.outskirtspress.com

Paperback ISBN: 978-1-4787-9558-2

Cover Photo © 2018 www.gettyimages.com. All rights reserved - used with permission.

Outskirts Press and the "OP" logo are trademarks belonging to Outskirts Press, Inc.

PRINTED IN THE UNITED STATES OF AMERICA

Contents

A Love Letter	1
A poets Inspiration	3
All I Know	4
Can I Be Your Man	6
Come To Me Baby	8
Come Walk With Me	10
Good God Girl, You're Rocking My World	12
Holding On	14
I Can't Help But Love You	16
I Want All Of You	18
I Wish	20
If I Were A Poet	22
In Love Forever	24
In The Middle of The Night	26
Inspired To Love	28
It's Time For Our Love	30
It's Time To Come Home Baby	32
Just a Glimpse of You	34
Just Love	36
Life as We Know It.	38
Love	40
Missing You	42
My Granny's Love	44
My Heart	46
My Lady Love	48
My Lady, My Woman, My Wife	50
My Last Love	52
No Words	54
Not Giving Up On Your Love	56
Of Her	58

On The Wings of Love	59
Ruky's Poem	61
Staying In The Love	63
Talking To You	65
The Love Poem	67
This Lovers Prayer	69
To Finally Find Love	71
To See You For The Very First Time	73
To The Woman That I Love	75
Today	77
Understanding	78
Walking Toward Your Love	80
We are Perfectly Perfect and I Wouldn't Change a Thing	82
What Can I Say About Love	84
What Is It	86
When I Knew That I Loved You	88
Where Do You Start	90
Why Do I Love You So	92
Why Does love Hurt	94
Your Sensuality	96

A Love Letter

My Dear Rukayatu
It seems as though we've never met.
But as plain as day, I see your face where ever I go.
I hear your voice calling my name.
I see the smile that drives me wild.

The love in your voice when we talk sends me to another place and time.
The heart that beats within your chest, God has truly blessed.
It is only with his help that a heart could hold so much love.
As for you and me, our hearts so freely we give one to the other.

Up until now the perfect match for our hearts had not been found.
Love has been built up and then torn down.
Those days and nights are well into the past never to be lived again.
Some how through all of the looking and searching,
I found you and you found me.

Rukayatu I'm writing this letter just to say, I need to be in your love
every night and everyday and I would have you to be in my love every night and every day.
I know that there are many miles and kilometers between us and today it's not possible for us to be together.

But the sun continues to shine to bring about that day
when not possible goes away.

Until that day I will dream about you whether I am awake
or sleep.
Until that day I will always listen to hear the voice of the one
who completes me.
Until that day my heart will keep seeking and seeking until
it finds yours.
Until that day my lips will continue to hunger and thirst just
for a taste of you.

In closing let me say this, when we're together there will be
no regrets, there will be no solitude, there will be no more
hurting hearts and there will be no more pain of loneliness.
There will only be one man loving one woman and one woman
loving one man throughout eternity.

A poets Inspiration

The color of your hair and the color of your eyes, the
tenderness in your smile incite me to write.
The words, your beauty pull from my heart,
they are poetic words and even some to me are new.

I listen closely to your voice, it's so pleasing to me.
And when you laugh music fills the air.
The way you care about others shows a soul not in despair.
But instead a soul that is happy to care.

The very image of you stir and move me to a place I've
never been.
A place where all is love, all is good and all is fair.
I can only imagine what to fill your presence would be like.

When thinking of you poetic words and rhymes fly through
the sky.
How could a poet not exclaim your deep beauty, your large
and loving heart.
How could a poet not say, she's like an angel walking in
our midst, spreading the blessings of love,
one to another.

To inspire a poet is like opening the shutters and letting the
light shine in.
To inspire a poet is to open the closed gates,
then and only then will words of such beauty and wisdom
fill the air, tugging on hearts and minds
every where.

All I Know

I know that the sun rises in the east and sets in the west.
I know that summers come and winters go.
I know that some birds sing and some birds chirp.
I know that in life, people come and people go.
That's all I know.

I know that in life sometimes, love comes and love goes.
I know that happy is a gift and that it's also, a state of being.
I know that hope can exist for all.
I know that to love is to live.
That's all I know.

I know that I love a woman who loves me so.
I know that her eyes can make me cry.
I know that looking at her lips makes me sigh.
I know that her voice is like music to my ears.
That's all I know.

I know that in her hands she holds my heart.
I know that her smile makes me feel like a child.
I know that her love is great and all encompassing.
I know that she gives to me all that she has to give.
That's all I know.

I know that the love my woman gives to me
Is like being in the land, of milk and honey.
I know that she knows, that I love her so.
I know that her heart is mine just as my heart is hers.
That's all I know.

I know that my heart is full, running over and bursting for her.
I know that my love will never go to another.
I know that when the sun no longer shines
and the moon no longer glows,
that I will still be loving her so.
That's all I know.

All I know is that she is for me and I am for her.
All I know is that we shall walk before God as a woman
and a man joined hand in hand and heart to heart.
All I know is that where she goes, I will go.
And that's, all I know.

Can I Be Your Man

Baby, I don't have diamonds or gold.
I don't drive a cadillac and I don't wear designer clothes.
I don't have a penthouse on time square
and I don't have a condo in the islands anywhere.

Baby, all those things that I don't have really don't mean a thing to me.
But the things that I do have I wouldn't trade for the world.

First and above all I have love in my heart.
Because I have love, faith always stands by my side.
Because I have love and faith,
hope decided to come along for the ride.

Now that love, faith and hope are always with me,
mercy has suddenly appeared.
Love, faith, hope and mercy,
those are the things that I own.

Love, faith hope and mercy they all live with me,
they are my charge, to show where ever I go.
Love being the greatest of all,
for without love, faith, hope and mercy could never exist.

My question to you baby is, can I be your man?
Can I walk with you holding your hand?
Can I take care of you when you need me to?
Can I love you just the way you want me to?

In this world there are not many things
that I wish for, that would be just for me.
But your love, I wish for whole heartedly,
and I want it to be, just for me.

You know the things that I don't have
as you know the things that I do possess.
My love for you burns deep within me
with an uncontrollable flame.
My heart calls your name
as it asks this question, baby, can I be your man?

Come To Me Baby

When we are alone in our home and my heart reaches for you,
these words you will hear me say.
Come to me baby, come to me and lets let our love fly.
Come to me my baby, and we will never let this love die.

When I look I can see my baby walking up to me.
As we walk together I can see her hand holding mine and I
can feel my heart skip with the beating of time.

Come to me baby, we will walk in the clouds with
our love right there between us, always holding us tight.
This life, this world, will all be ours on that certain night
when we come together and we let our love take to flight.

Come to me my baby, come to me my love,
all of the obstacles that have been between us
have fallen one by one. Now only one more stands,
as I remove it from our path surely there can be
no doubt or wonder about how deep my love is for you.

Come to me and we shall do the undoable, we will hear the
un-hearable, we will see the unseeable
and will touch the untouchable.
These doors, our love opens for us,
we need but to step through.

A new life awaits us,
come to me my baby and we will let it take us.
A new love, a new life, a new joy and a new happiness
all these things are ours to have and to hold

from that first day forward when to each other we give
our love.

Come to me my love, my sweetheart, my darling,
let us show God the Father that we honor the
abundant blessings, that upon us, he has bestowed.
The love that he has given us to share is not just an
ordinary love.
It transcends all the known concepts of this worlds love.

Come to me baby, that's all you need do.
Come to me baby, and all of our wishes and dreams will
come true.

Come Walk With Me

Come walk with me to places beyond the stars.
Come walk with me and hold my hand.
Come walk with me and stand by your man.
Come walk with me says my heart to your heart.
The stars are in the hand of the man that has your heart.
Come walk with me my true love, Rukayatu.

Come walk with me to a thousand places that we've never seen.
Come walk with me to the corners of our hearts.
Come walk with me and let us find together loves deepest pleasures.
Come walk with me I want you always by my side.
Come walk with me my darling through this life and all others.
Come walk with me the dream of my dreams, Rukayatu.

Come walk with me through all the moments of time.
Come walk with me in our one and only love.
Come walk with me and always be mine.
Come walk with me my baby you are the only one that my heart wants.
Come walk with me to the other side of the street where flowers grow and love flows.
Come walk with me my loving sweetheart, Rukayatu.

Together, our love will out last the flames of a burning sun.
Together, our hearts will heal all wounds of the past.
Together, our minds will clearly see each other as it was meant to be.

Together, our souls belong because there's no telling one from the other.
Come walk with me the woman who makes my heart to beat, Rukayatu.

If I had to climb a thousand mountains to get to you I would.
If I had to fight tooth and nail to be by your side I would.
If I had to give all that I have to love you and only you I would.
If I had to spend a thousand sleepless nights just to spend one night with you I would.
If I had to shout of my love for you to the whole world I would.
Come walk with me for you are the stars in my sky, Rukayatu.

Come walk with me the loveliest of them all.
Come walk with me the one who makes my heart fly.
Come walk with me the one who sets my soul on fire.
Come walk with me my hearts desire.
Come walk with me and others our love will inspire.
Come walk with me that we may be as one.
Come walk with me my lady, my lover, my woman and my wife, Rukayatu.

Good God Girl, You're Rocking My World

A love like yours is all most impossible to find.
A woman with a heart so pure and clean
that it makes the angels sing.

A woman whose care and love runs deep like the sea.
Your love has changed my world and made it a better place
to be.
You are a woman whose intellect exceeds that of most men,
just because of the contents of your heart.

Your love when you give it is a take all or nothing deal.
As for love, of your self you give freely and of your own will.
A love like yours is meant to be honored and cherished for
there are few if any whose love can equal to yours.

The more that I love you, the more you make me love you.
The things that you say and do let me know that your love is
oh so true.
If there were ever a vision of an angel dancing around in
my head, I already know, the vision would be of you.

In your arms I rock back and forth my dear,
wrapped in your love, bliss and harmony.
I lay there rocking with your arms surrounding me, the
rocking is slow, calm and gentle.

I can feel all of your love and care.
I can feel the beating of your heart

because your love has conquered me
even though I gave up without a fight.

If I could have anything that I wanted in this world, It would always be you.
If I could walk with just one person for the rest of my days,
It would always be you.
If I could talk with only one person for the rest of my life,
that person would be you.
If I was forced to dream only one dream from now until
eternity, that dream would only be of you.

If there were no hands on a clock
and there was no time to tell,
forever through this life we would sail.

In respect of how I feel about your love,
I'll just say this again,
Good God Girl, You're Rocking My World!

Holding On

I'm holding on to your love, I'm holding on to you forever.
Sometimes when our eyes can't see we still have to be,
holding on.
And during those times when with our ears we don't hear,
we still need to be, holding on.

When you have something that eludes most in their life time,
treat it as the rarest treasure and just keep, holding on.
When some would have you fight, look into the eyes of
each other and just keep, holding on.

When the world would tear us apart for one reason or
another, let our grips on each other grow in strength
as we just keep , holding on.
Some will say that our love will not last, while others will
look and see, just how tightly, we keep, holding on.

When a once in a life time love finally comes along,
If you really do want it, you better be, holding on.
It's easy to let the best things that have ever happened to us
just kinda slip away and after they're gone, we realize just
how important it is to just keep, holding on.

Your love to me is more precious than all the air in the sky
and all the waters in the seas, that's why you will always
find me, tightly, holding on.
My love, your way it runs. It leaves my heart with haste,
rushing, so that in your heart it may find a place.

Without you my soul would be empty and my heart barren of
feelings and love.
For me the light of day would be gone
and all that would be left is the darkest of nights.
My mind would be desolate of loving thoughts and
forever wants.

When the love of others has grown cold and fallen away,
because we're holding on, our love will remain strong.
Our love will survive the test of time.
Our love will never end.
Just because we never stopped, to each other, holding on.

I Can't Help But Love You

When I am at a loss for words, one glimpse of you will do
what ten thousand thoughts couldn't do.
The door to my heart flies open and
words begin to soar.

Sometimes it's hard to get the heart and the mind
exactly where they need to be to release creativity.
Especially when loves involved, the mind sometimes
feel like it's a ping pong ball.

My heart wonders, what's up with love any way?
Is it here to stay or is it going to run away?
Is it here that it will abide or will it just go and hide?
Will love give to me what I need or will it not care and
cease to be.

Love can give and love can take away.
It can give a man his hearts desire.
It can also leave that man in a puddle of misery and pain.
Love is love, it has nothing to lose or to gain.

My mind asks, what's up with that thing called love any
way?
It can rush in like a whirl wind claiming all within it's reach.
Then suddenly it's gone leaving behind
a menagerie of things tossed aside.

If you are in love and want to be in love
climb into that saddle, dig your knees in real deep.

Ride with determination and tenacity
until love no longer tries to buck you off.

Always remember that any thing worth having is
worth waiting for and fighting for when necessary.
We cannot conquer love because it cannot be
bound, tied down or locked up.
We can only climb aboard for the ride.

I can't help but love you
no matter what love decides to do.
Because for me there is only you.

I Want All Of You

I want you morning noon and night.
The things that you do to me make me want you more and more.
The way that you look, when you know that I know, that you're looking at me.
And when you I see you, I always smile and say, my baby.

If I wanted to name all the things that I love about you
I would soon run out of words because the number is so great.
But I will name a few just for you.

I love all the lines and curves of your face.
I love your eyes because they always seem to be focused on me.
I love your beautiful smile, it drives me wild.
I love your long glistening hair it truly is your glory.
I love each and ever curve of your body
and I love the fact that God made you, just the right height for me.

All the things that I just named, they anyone can plainly see.
But the greatest beauty of you lies with inside.
It resides in that place that no one can see
and access is only granted, when you want it to be.

But baby I'm not the type to pick and choose so I'll just say it plainly, I want all of you.
I want the woman that I see.
And I want her to forever, be with me.

It's astonishing how much beauty and love one person
can hold.
All the things that are good, God wrapped them with you.
When you love, you love with all that you have in your heart.
And you know that your love, is only yours to give.

I want to walk hand in hand with the woman who loves me.
I want to look into your eyes straight into your soul
and see why God gave you to me.
That day, blessed me, he did, with a forever love, to call
my own.

My love for you is like a hunger that grows deeper and
stronger.
It drives me to want you endlessly.
For my heart, my love and my soul, I can truly speak
and say, baby, we want all of you.

I Wish

I wish that I had been the one who always wiped the teardrops from your eyes.
I wish that I had been the one who always made you laugh and smile.
I wish that I had always been the one that filled your heart with love.
I wish that I had always been the one that you called your man.

I wish that I had been the first to ever hold your hand.
I wish that I had been the first and only one to ever kiss your lips.
I wish that I had been the first to caress and hold you so close to me.
I wish that I had been the first that you gave your love to.

I wish that in my life I had only known you.
I wish that in my life no time had been wasted on love that wasn't the right love.
I wish that my days and nights had always been filled with you.
I wish that my heart had always belonged to you.

I wish that my heart had always known the love of you.
I wish that my mind had always known the existence of you.
I wish that my love I had always given freely to you.
I wish that my hands had always known to reach for you.

Now I wish that your love never stops holding me tight.
Now I wish that forever my lips will be the only ones to steal your kiss.

Now I wish for loving you every day and every night.
Now I wish that I could hear you just call my name.

Lives are full of wishes just as they are full of dreams.
No one should wish their life away just for the sake of
wishing or dream their life away
just for the sake of dreaming.

But it is always good to dream of or wish for the one that
you love.
It is always good to dream of warm and tender nights.
It is also good to wish for the one who is your lover, your
woman, your wife.

Today I wish to be your only love.
Today I wish to be the only one who will ever kiss your lips.
Today I wish to be the only one to whom you give your
loves hug.
Today I wish to see this love that is between us in each
others eyes.
Today I wish to see the smile that's only for me.
Today I wish to hold the hands of the one who I love so
dearly.
Today I wish that I could fly across the sky and land where
you are and do all the things that this day,
I have wished for.

If I Were A Poet

If I were a poet I would use words of rhyme to tell about this love of mine.
If I were a poet all the words would be spoken just at the right time.
If I were a poet the spaces between the lines is where my message you would find.
If I were a poet my words would be crystal clear even to the blind.

If I were a poet I would say of thee, you are more than just a mere person.
If I were a poet my words would tell the untold story of your endless beauty.
If I were a poet I would say that your eyes show where your love goes.
If I were a poet I would tell of the beauty of your hair, so long and fair, it's your glory that you wear.

If I were a poet in love with you what more could I say than, it's of you that I dream.
If I were a poet that has given you his heart I would say, my darling, it is with you that I'm in love.
If I were a poet who's deeply in love with you, I would say words that are filled with love, hope and devotion.

If I were a poet, in your ear, these words you would hear.
You are my Lady, woman, wife and Queen.
You are the songs that I sing.

Know that day breaks just to be close to you
and night falls in an attempt to cover you with it's loving dew.

If I were a poet my words would say, you are my love,
my life, my heart and my soul,
to all of these the key you hold.
If I were a poet my words would caress you every night and
never let you go.
If I were a poet on my knees is where I would be,
shouting of my undying love for thee.

If I were a poet you would be the words of my every
spoken line.
If I were a poet you would be my only word for love.
If I were a poet my heart and soul would always be at
your door.
If I were a poet with no more words to give, my heart
would fly from my chest and land upon your breasts.

If I were your poet my heart would every day sing.
If I were your poet love from the mountain tops would ring.
If I were your poet my words would be as sweet as a kiss
form your lips.
If I were your poet, to make you happy,
words would only be my second set of tools.

In Love Forever

As the winds of time blow and things that we know change
as our lives keep marching forward, whether there is love
or not.
Days and nights, they come and they go. As our world turns,
there seems to be nothing permanent and stedfast.

As we look around to see what we can see, we glance to the
heavens and the things that we see,
the sun, the moon and all the twinkling stars.
Nothing that we see there shall last forever.
The mountains, though they be strong and tall, they too,
shall one day fall.

If nothing is permanent and stedfast, then why do we exist
in its midst.
If there is nothing solid to which we can hold on to
then why are we so bold as to live on.
Life is precious, that much we know.

But why is life so precious?
Is it because of our loved ones or all the games and fun?
Do we hold this life as precious because we can see, hear,
feel, speak and touch.
Life is so precious because, it is life, where were you, before
you were born?

Now to bring it back from the deep.
Life and love are the only two eternal things.
Both of these we have been given.
Then suddenly grace appeared on the wings of love,

for after all, we are only, man and woman.

To go a little further, I would say that love is the key to life everlasting.
To be deep rooted in love forever is where we all need to be.
The gift of these two, life and love, have forever shaped our world.
We can live, die and live again just because of the
great love passed to us, from the Fathers hand.

For me to be in love forever, I must see, that which is most important to me.
For me to be in love forever, I must believe, that I'm not a lone,
there must be others with love, running through their bones.
For me to be in love forever is it just faith that I need,
or is it faith, hope and charity.

Love was here before it all and love will be here after it's gone.
So If you live in love forever and if the one that you love,
loves you back, you will never be alone,
because in love forever, you have found your home.

In The Middle of The Night

In the middle of the night holding you tight,
kissing your lips and feeling your heart beat.

I can see your eyes in the dark filled with love and joy.
I feel your hands touching me anywhere they can.
I feel the impulse of your shallow breath on my neck.

In the middle of the night I can hold your face in my hands
while I kiss your lips.
I will run my fingers through your hair as I rub your head
and look into your eyes through the darkness of night.

As my hands glide over you, my mind, heart and soul all
collide.
Feelings and emotions and desires fly every where, in the
middle of the night.
As we get closer and closer until there is no space between us,
then we become as one, in life and in love.

As we lay there together feeling and absorbing each others
passion our hearts melt together to never be parted.
With loves sweet embrace we cling to each other
as if we fear loosing the greatest thing we've ever had.

In the middle of the night our love grows stronger and
stronger until it explodes because it's finally found
the place that makes it whole.

When love comes to us in the middle of the night
we will grab hold and hang on tight.
We will hold each other in the arms of love,
and this love we will never let go of.

In the middle of the night as I call your name
my tender loving heart will never be the same.
It will be more tender and more loving and more caring
and forever needing and wanting to call your name.

In the middle of the night where our dreams rule,
love will always find us, still holding, each other tight.

Inspired To Love

You have inspired me to love again,
after saying that I never would.
Just one look into yours eyes is all it took.
I could see for myself all that you had been through and the
toll that you had paid.

And likewise my heart was battered, bruised, and beaten.
It had suffered wounds that I thought would never heal.
But then along came you, within your eyes I saw you smile.
Your smile reflected that which lies deep inside of you.

Your beauty does not stop at the surface of the skin.
That's just where it begins.
The deeper and deeper I look into your soul
the more and more your beauty grows.

You have inspired me to love again
and with myself to be friends.
To love others you must first,
love yourself.

You have done more than to inspire me to love again,
you have inspired me to live again.
My world and my life are new just because of you.
You have given me the greatest reason for living, your love.

You give your love to me as I give my love to you.
We don't look back because we're going forward.
We don't carry baggage from the past, just love for our future.

You have inspired me to be who I really am,
a warm hearted and loving man.

All I have to do is look at your face,
I feel my love, your love and our love,
all in the same place.

You have inspired me my darling,
you have given me the hope that I need.
I am inspired to love only you.
I am inspired to love again just because of you.

It's Time For Our Love

As I sit and think of you and our love that is forever true,
my mind searches for the reasons why our love will not die.
Our love was sent from above to be forged in earthly fire.
Love that has been tempered and hardened by the flame
will not bend, break or shatter, it will always hold the shape
in which it was forged.

Every day because of the forging flames, our love gets a little
harder and more steadfast in our hearts as we never,
allow it to change.
As our love stands against all the things that come against us,
it refuses to bend, break or shatter.

As I sat I continued to think about you and our love that is
forever true.
And in my mind I could hear a voice say to me,
why do you look back at the past without even realizing it?
Yesterday was not the time for the love that I have given to
both of you, nor was last year or last century.

Then I knew, that now, is the time for our love.
Now I know, that it makes no sense to look back and think
about what may have been.
Today, right now, I know that, it's time for our love.

Our love is for now and the future, not the past.
That makes our gift of love so much more special.
It didn't have to be you and me that fell so deeply in love.

It didn't have to be you and me that found so much favor in his sight.

But it is you and me that have been blessed, with this love to see.
This love because of it's magnitude causes us so much pain, but neither one us, wants that to change.
This love God gave to you and me, and in doing so, he set us both free.

The chains and the shackles have fallen away from our hearts.
And know this, that the deceiver of the world is not happy with us.
For our love runs like a river, giving love and hope and encouragement, to those who need it most.
And this the whole world will see.

It seem as though our love is out front in the battle between love and hate.
When our love is placed on the scale, it tips the weight to favor love instead of hate.
So through it all, our love we must uphold.
We must always know and remember that now, it's time for our love.

It's Time To Come Home Baby

It's time for you to come home baby, you been gone way
too long.
It seems like you been gone forever.
I eat alone, I drink alone and I sleep alone
every since you been gone.

I find myself fighting off this love jones everyday.
It's like I can see you, I can touch you
and I can even smell the sweetness of your scent.
But then I realize with great dismay, that you're not here.

It's time for you to come home baby, you been gone way
too long.
When was the last time I kissed your lips?
When was the last time that I held and rubbed your soft and
tender hands.
When was the last time that you looked into my eyes and
smiled at me.

My heart says never and my mind says, maybe ever!
That's what you do to me baby, when you leave me all
alone.
I try to be strong like the man that I am,
but your love makes me so weak in the knees.

I miss you so much baby, If I wasn't a man I'd cry.
Because everyone knows that a man is not suppose to cry.
I just wish that somebody would tell that to my eyes.

It's time for you to come home baby, you been gone way
too long.
My lips miss all your tender kisses.
My arms miss the caress, from them, you always get.
My eyes wish and wish and wish that they could
behold your beauty, once again, in their sight.

If I had a magic wand I would waive it just for fun.
The first wish that I would grant would be my own,
my wish, to have you hear at home.

I know, that you now, that I know, your love, I have.
You know ,that I know, that you know, my love, you have.
No matter where ever we are our love is alway together.
But it's time for you to come home baby, you been gone way
to long.
Bring my love home to me baby, because your love, is here
waiting.

Just a Glimpse of You

If I could have but only one glimpse of you.
If I could only see the smile that mesmerizes me.
If I could only feel the brush of your gentle touch.
If I could only be the shirt on your back baby.

With just a glimpse of your love my heart cry's out,
Please, please love me!
With just a glimpse of you the sun has no choice but to rise.
When compared to your radiant beauty the moon
must run and hide.

The most beautiful flowers hesitate to bloom,
when you're in the room.
The loveliness of you captivates and the
fullness of your beauty simply inebriates.

If my eyes could see forever or just behold a glimpse of you
in a fleeting moment of time.
They would search high and low,
just to find that one glimpse, of your tantalizing beauty.

If I could, I would hold the beauty of your heart locked
inside of me where there is no key.
If I could, I would mingle the beauty of your thoughts with
my own.
If I could, I would conquer and cherish the beauty of your love.

A glimpse of your beauty would be all that I'd need
to walk with my head in the clouds.

A glimpse of your love would to my heart sing
a thousand songs of your unequaled beauty.

Just a glimpse of you and I would leap for joy.
Just a glimpse of you would turn my heart into your toy.
Just a glimpse of you would make my world go around.
Just a glimpse of you would exclaim your beauty
without ever making a sound.

Just Love

What can it be that makes the world turn round and round!
What can it be that never makes a sound.
What can it be that keeps the oceans and the seas at bay for you and me.
What can it be that makes the sun and the moon both shine.
What can it be that makes the rain fall from the sky.
What can it be that moves the heart of people like you and I,
just Love.

Love has no beginning, it has always been.
Love has no ending because it just begins again.
Love cannot be hidden because if it's there it over flows.
Love respects not a person for their title or rank.
Love gives and gives and gives.
Love cannot be silenced or quieted down,
after all, love never makes a sound.
What does it take to truly set mankind free,
just love.

In our hearts we know that if pain is not healed it will surely grow.
In our hearts we also know that sorrow will over shadow all,
if love is never called.
In our minds live thoughts of this life and the next,
what if there is no love that was ever given.
What if love doesn't really exist.
Fear not, we have a guarantee that was paid for
back on calvary.
You may ask what was the cost to acquire this guarantee,
and the answer would be,
just love.

Can't you see, that life is given as a gift to all who live.
This life will one day pass away but the gift of life eternal
is there to stay.
It's also given freely to those who love God's way.
How can this be, is there really life eternally,
do the birds really fly in the sky and do fish really swim in
the sea.
How can all these things be?
They are, because God is.
They are because God wanted it to be so.
For God so loved mankind that he paid the ransom for
our eternal lives and the cost was,
just love.

Life as We Know It.

Day will break and the sun will shine.
Stormy clouds will run sometimes.
Winter brings ice and snow.
Spring is when things begin to grow.

All these things we expect in this life because that's what we know.
We know that the rain falls from the sky.
We know that the wind blows.
We know that colors are different and some even glow.

So whats the key to the mystery?
What's the key to why we are here.
Is it written down in a book or told in tales?
Who can stand and testify that this life is not, a heaven or a hell?

This life is as we know it and that's all that we know.
No one can stand, raise their hand and say, they asked to come here.
The choice was not ours to make.
We searchingly cry, Why and When, did it all begin?

The answer has always been staring us dead in the face.
Mostly we choose to look away.
The answer even calls our name and we choose not to hear.
The answer tells us that if we look we will be able see.

Life as we know it for each of us one day will cease to be.
We that have looked and have seen, know that it's not the end, but just the beginning.

Some of us go which ever way the wind blows, running to
and fro.
Never stopping to think, is this really the way that I should go?

The key to the door that solves the mystery
is in each one of our hands.
You don't have to work for it and doesn't cost a thing.
Its not heavy to lift or awkward to hold.
Just stretch out your hands one to another
and pass God's love all around.

Love

Love is sometimes all that you can say,
for some love has the power to make them do wrong, but for
others love has the power to make them do right.

Love is a mysterious thing it can come and go
and can never really ever have meant a thing.
But on the other hand, love is the most precious of gems.
When there is that type of love, the angels in heaven sing of it.

The latter is the love that I have for you.
Of this love that I have for you, there will never be a sequel.
This love, has no equal.

Love can give you happiness
and love can take it away.
But to live in love is a glorious thing.
No greater happiness have I ever seen.

I tell you that I love you
and you tell me the same.
When we live in love there is
only happiness to gain.

My love for you is strong and masculine.
Your love for me is true and feminine.
Those two loves together
create a love that is strong and true.

My love for you at times literally take my breath away.
My heart feels for you

the greatest feelings of all, a love thats true.

I really don't know what to say
that would make you see the love thats in me.
I really don't know what to do or to say
other than that which I've already said and done.

My love for you requires of me
to always do what is best for you.
Not just because its whats best for you
but because, I love you.

Missing You

You've been gone from home one day
and I just can't say how I'm missing you.
I look for the sound of your words that to me are so familiar.

But there are no words from which
to make the sounds
because my girls gone way out of town.

Back to me one day she will come
but until then I can only say, I'm missing you.
I miss you most early in the morning and late at night
when we should be in each others arms holding on tight.

In my mind I can see you and even hear your voice,
I reach out to touch you but you're not there,
that's when I really start missing you.

I miss talking to you baby both day and night.
I miss the sound of your voice and your laughter.
I also miss the way you say the name, Kerry.
I guess I could just simply say, baby, I'm missing you.

The word missing tells the whole story,
here it denotes that one is gone from the other.
Because of the love that we have
the missing doesn't travel just one way,
I know that you are missing me just as much as I am
missing thee.

I miss the smile that I know is on your face
when I say something to make you laugh.
I miss the feelings of your happiness
when I have done something to make you happy.

I miss the way that you say that you love me.
I miss the way that I could almost hold your heart in my
hands when we spoke of our love and passion for each
other.

I guess I might as well just say, I love everything about you
and everything about you, I'm missing this day.
Because my love for you is so great
my heart will not be content unless I tell you, I'm missing you.

My Granny's Love

I remember my granny, the only one that I ever knew.
She was small in stature, but to me she stood 6 feet tall.
I would often catch a glimpse of my granny after she had
gone, just by seeing a reflection of her
in the face of my mother.

My granny's love for me was solid, sound and strong.
She had her own special name for me
and I still wonder how that came to be.
Just like my mother, my granny, truly loved me.

I can still see here in my mind, I can still hear her voice
calling me by my special name.
My granny loved and revered our God.
She lived by his word and his love.

My granny was the mother of ten children who all save one
have lived long and happy lives.
My granny was the strength in the family,
she always knew what was wrong and what was right.

I never saw my granny withhold love from anyone
and I never saw her refuse to help anyone in need.
I always felt lucky that my granny, belonged to me.

My granny was the daughter of a happily married white
man and black woman.
She was born at the the turn of the 20th century.
As it was then, so it is now, love knows no boundaries
or shame, love only knows, that it loves.

My granny's heart was shaped and molded by God and
his word.
My grandfather loved her with his whole heart
and would have given her the world if he could.
When my grandfather passed away
they had been married for 63 years.

My granny's love to me was a safe place to run and hide
from anyone or anything.
While playing out side at her house one day, at the age of 4, I
was attacked by a rooster and I ran crying to my granny.
All I can say is that those were the best
chicken and dumplings ever,
that we ate for supper that day.

My Heart

How do you explain your heart to the one that you love
with words that would be understood.
Maybe you could say that my heart was conceived
in pure and true love.
A love that stood the test of time, it never died or ceased to be.

My heart was made to love and to love deeply.
My heart entered this world already filled
and running over with love un-paralleled.
The heart that is within me only seeks to find it's one true love.

My heart has aches and pains just like every other heart.
But my heart, because it loves so deeply,
those aches and pains are all ten fold.

My heart gives of it's self all that there is to give
when it feels that it has found that one love that was made
just for it.
My heart has felt happiness and sadness, love and despair,
joy and loneliness, peace and turmoil.

My heart has survived till this day because of the love that
God sent to me through my parents.
My heart is soft and tender it doesn't like things that hurt
others.
My heart cries when it sees things that are not good or right
and it wonders why.

When my heart runs to someone I surely listen
because it knows the heart for which it has been looking.

My heart has a mind of it's own
it knows to whom it should belong.

Rukayatu, my heart has ran to you.
Rukayatu, from all others my heart has picked you.
Rukayatu, my heart now belongs to only you.

My heart is full of the love that I have for you.
My heart hears, sees or feels for no other.
In you my heart has found the one and only love
about which it gives a damn.

The feelings that I have for you are unexplainable.
Your love never leaves me to be alone.
It reaches out and touches me from afar.
Maybe that's because, Rukayatu, you are my heart.

My Lady Love

Maybe I can sneak a hug and steal a kiss form those vibrant lips.
Or maybe I will whisper your name as I pass by and you'll notice me from all the other guys.

If I only knew what to do when I'm close to you.
I want so badly to run my fingers through your hair.
I dream of how it would be, just a touch, between you and me.

If I could just walk with you as though we were just a woman and a man.
If I could just see the beauty of my baby.
I long to hear words straight from your lips
and all the little sounds that you make.

If I could only touch the heart of my lady love
the light in my life would be brighter than bright.
If I could sing, I would sing the greatest love song
of all times, just for you.

If I could wish upon a single shooting star,
my wish would be, for you to always love me.
Nor by might or will can I see beyond you into the future.
But what I do see, today and now, this love, we both want and need.

My lady love gives her love to me
and I accept it with overwhelming glee.
My lady love you are the light of life that walks with me.

If I could be any man that I wanted to be
I would only want to be the man, that your love sees.
I would fight ten thousand battles
and sleigh a thousand dragons just to hold you in my arms,
my lady love.

When I see the look of love in yours eyes, just for me,
my heart shakes and trembles and I think
oh, how I would love to be able to let my love quench your desires.

If I could only be the man that you see.
If I could only be the hand that you hold.
If I could only be the flame that heats up your soul.
I want my heart to always hold, all the love
that you have to give , you are the lady, of my love.

My Lady, My Woman, My Wife

Your love my Lady surrounds me.
Your love my Lady engulfs my soul.
Your beauty my Lady stuns me.
Your beauty my Lady kindles the fires of my love.

Your heart my Lady is more precious than gold.
Your heart my Lady holds my very soul.
Your heart my Lady makes my heart smile.
Your heart my Lady gives love for more than just a little while.

I know that you are my Woman.
The only person who really knows me is my Woman.
My Woman knows just what to say when I need a word of calm.
My Woman sees that which lies deep in side of me.

The Woman that I love is my Woman.
The Woman to whom I give all of me is my Woman.
The Woman who loves me more than any other is my Woman.
My Woman's love fits me like a glove, because she's, my Woman.

When I found my Lady and my Woman happy was I,
because my Lady and my Woman where one in the same.
I love my Lady and my Woman from head to toe.
Without my Lady and my Women I'd wonder which way to go.

When a man finds the one his heart clings to he had best take notice.

When a man only wants to talk to just this one.
When a man wants to love her forever deep and passionately.
When a man misses her presence so badly that it hurts.

When a man has found his Lady and his Woman,
he would be a fool if he didn't make her his Wife.
A Wife to love and to hold on those long cold nights.
A Wife that loves him more than life.
She is already his Lady and his Woman
and now, she will be his Wife.

My Last Love

For a life time it seems that love comes and love goes.
I have loved before and it has always seemed to fail.
Was it me, was it her or was it just the world.
Love lost can very seldom be again found.

I have loved and I have lost.
I have cared to see my feelings brushed aside.
I have given all that I had to give.
It wasn't enough to keep love from running away.

In my heart I know the pain of love lost.
In my mind spins the wheel of time.
My thoughts are sometimes of what love used to be.
But now my thoughts are of the love that I now see.

I see a love so deep and so strong.
I see a love greater than any that I have known.
I see my love, my woman, my wife.
I see the last love of my life.

This love that I have found is the love
on which my world evolves around.
This love shines with the brightest of light.
This love carries me to places unseen.
This is more than just a dream, it holds my soul,
my heart and my inner being.

For the love of her I would do anything.
For the love of her my life would I give.
For the love of her my heart will always sing.
For the love of her my hands will always reach.

As I walk this world there is no other perfect girl.
For someone to love I will not look or search again.
In her heart she holds the key to my happiness.
In her heart I am held tight and secure.

When I look into her eyes I see, my last love.
When I hold her hand I feel the touch of the one that I want to be, my last love.
When I see her lips I want them to be the last lips to press against mine.
When I look into her eyes that final time before I fly away, I will gently say, you are, my last love.

No Words

No words have ever been spoken that can explain your beauty.
No words known to man can describe the depth and breadth of your love.
Words shiver and run away when ever your heart is mentioned, that's a task they don't want to have to face.

No words carry a sound with which to expound on the inner qualities of you.
There are no words to tell of the pain and sorrow that you have felt.
There are no words able to say that your heart wasn't truly broken.
If only there were words that could really comfort and heal.

If only there were words that could tell just how much you care.
There are many words, but none exist that can tell of your loving, loving bliss.
As for me, I've never heard a word say, I don't want her to stay.

No words, no words are willing to say, just how much, your love is real.
No words can ever say, just how much of yourself you give everyday.
No words even care to try and explain, the look in your eyes, for your man.
No words, no words for you my love, not even from, the heavens above.

I have no words to explain, the love that I feel for her, it's just not the same.
Words, words, if only they could explain the smile inside your eyes.
If only words could explain, those lips that are so, so tender.
If only there were words to explain, your expression, that's burned into my brain.

If only words could tell of the feelings that I feel when I'm thinking of you.
I know of no words that can explain the feeling in my heart, that's not pain.
Her smile leaves me speechless, there are no words to say.
The need to reach out and touch her grows stronger and stronger day by day.
But yet there are still no words to say.

If there are words capable of describing and telling of her, those words I want to be the first to hear.
I will keep them in my heart and forever hold them dear.

This poem was written for Rukayatu Suleiman Irons. After all, you don't speak of a woman this way and not say her name.

Not Giving Up On Your Love

Under no circumstances, no ifs, no ands, or buts
will I ever give up on your love.
There is no power on this earth that can tear
my love away from you.

A foolish man would I be, if after finding the love that I need
and the love that needs me, to even consider turning and
walking away.
Where we are now in our lives, we have come together, you
and I.
Theres nothing in the past that holds any interest for me.

The future is all that I see and in that future I see you and me.
I see us hand in hand and your heart with my heart.
I see you and me as we always will be,
loving each other through out eternity.

Just be still for a moment and feel my love deep inside of
you.
Listen to the beats of our hearts as they tell each other, I've
been looking for you.
To walk away from your love under any terms would be the
act of brainless moron.

I'm not giving up on your love baby.
I'm not giving up on you and me.
I refuse to let our dreams of love,
joy, happiness just fade away.

I refuse to say good bye to the one and only one that I love.
I refuse to return to that empty life when there was no you.
I refuse to look away from your love, in it I must stay.
I refuse to have an empty heart when it can be filled with you.

It's not in my DNA to give up or run away
form something that I really, really want.
Here, now and for every hour to come
that something is you baby.

I pray and I thank the Father above
for the favor in me he found
and gave me your love.
No, I will never give up on your love,
then what would I be, just me, in a world filled with misery.

Of Her

I think of her constantly.
My mind is where I find
all the things that I know of her.
My soul holds tightly the essence of her.
My heart longs for any part of her.

With extreme desire I want to know the scent of her.
With anticipation my hands want to know the feel of her.
My lips are eager to know the taste of her.

My eyes have yet to see the radiant beauty of her.
My arms have yet to hold and feel the softness of her.
My heart has yet to rejoice at the mere presence of her.

My love has not yet tasted the sweetness of her.
My thoughts are full with pictures of her.
My dreams are filled with all things of her.

My days and nights are all about thinking of her.
My heart is bound by the magic of her.
My life is worth living just because of her.

My existence makes sense because of her.
My world has gone from dark to light because of her.
My face always has a smile just because of her.

The moon rises and floats across the sky because of her, the tides of the oceans and seas rise and fall just because of her. All of my stars twinkle and glisten, at the sight of her.

On The Wings of Love

Grace, hope and life all flew down from heaven
on the wings of love.
Into Mary's womb Jesus flew
on the wings of love.

When God sends his peace and comfort
to all of those who would accept it,
he sends them on the wings of love

We all live on the battle field between good and evil.
God loves those who stand for what's right and good in his
sight.
Sometimes it seems that evil is winning the fight,
but then I remember, God is my help and Jesus
is my shield.

God created man form the clay and dust of this earth.
He than breathed the breath of life into him.
God sent that breath from him to man,
on the wings of love.

I send to the woman that I love sole proprietorship
of my heart, my mind, my body and my soul.
And yes, they're all being delivered,
on the wings of love,

On the wings of love,
I send peace and good will to every
man, women and child,
who are all, Gods creations.

On the wings of love,
it would be okay for man to send
God's love to one another.

On the wings of love some things
should never cease to fly,
such as forgiveness, caring, sympathy, empathy,
understanding and the desire
to help anyone in need.

Ruky's Poem

As I take pen to paper let it be known that these words
can never be undone, now and forever will they be
immortalized.

I can see the contents of your heart just by looking at your face.
There lies the truth about you. The truth about how you love,
the truth about how you care and the truth about
how you give of yourself to others.

Your face is but a sign, showing all the beauty of mankind.
Now that I know those things which live in your heart and
soul, if I didn't already have your love
I would beg for it constantly.
Your words baby, they speak truth and testify to the love
that is in you.

If I could own the whole world or just your love, the world
would never be mine.
As you are , we all should be, humble enough to show
humility.
For that's the side of man that God loves to see.
To be humble to God and his love is a blessed women's trait.

Yes my darling Ruky, you are the same as me. We have been
blessed by our God
because this love that we have for each other, he can plainly
see.

This love that spans the ocean, flies through time, soars to
the heavens and then rests, at his feet.

If there were ever a love to be proclaimed, it is ours.
If there were ever a love to be heralded, it is ours.
If there were ever a woman who deserves
the truest love that a man could ever give, she, is you.

My Ruky, your heart is like no others woman's heart.
Your love is like no other woman's love.
But then the angels didn't have time
to give the perfect heart and the perfect love to everyone.

I can see the love all over your face.
I can see the love on your lips when they smile.
I can see the love in your eyes just from your gaze.
I can see my love that you have taken inside.

For me my darling, love is the eternal portrait of you.
Joy and happiness are just the residuals of being near you.
I pray that hope and faith in our love will never give way.
To me my love you are the essence of the beginning of true
beauty.

Staying In The Love

Sometimes we have to make sure that with all the things
that are going on around us and in our lives,
that we don't lose our focus and that our eyes remain on
the prize.
This love that we have been blessed with, should never be
taken for granite.

To this love, we should always be willing to give our all.
In this love, we both should be living.
Everyday, morning and night, this love needs to be held
tight.
If this love that we have is done right, it cannot help
but to grow strong and tall, every day and every night.

Today there are many things in our lives that are trying to
pull us apart.
We must take heed to these things and deal with them as
they come.
But the most important thing to us
must be, staying in the love.

Some may ask, how do you stay in the love?
To stay in the love you only need to remember,
that very first look or that very first touch
or that very first kiss or the first time,
you heard words, from each other lips.

If you hunger for that touch.
If you long to see that smile.
If your heart drags the ground when you are apart.

Because of these things you are walking, talking
and living in the love.

The secret to staying in the love, is to
there, always want to be.
When you're staying in the love
it doesn't matter about the things that may come or go.

If I could have but one wish from you,
it would be, that with me, you walk this land
hand in hand and that we would always
be found, staying in the love.

And after all the trials and tribulations
of our love are done,
that we still be, in this love,
that was meant, for just you and me.

Talking To You

I love you, is what I say when I'm talking to you.
You are a must be in my life just like the air that I breath.
The coolness of your breeze and the warmness of your touch,
to me would be all that I need.

My eyes constantly look at your likeness
and my heart is filled with desire.
My desire runs deeper than just a simple want.
My desire for you is like a flame
that forever burns and never goes out.

I love you, is what I say when I'm talking to you.
I love you, is what I say when my heart tells me to.
I love you, is what I say to you,
even when I'm feeling sad and blue.

My love for you never stops,
it never rests and it never takes a break.
My love for you is the only constant in my life.
I can depend on it because its always true.

When I look into your eyes I'm talking to you,
telling you that, I love you.
When I would hold your hand I'm talking to you,
telling you that, I love you.

Those three simple words that I say to you
are like the keys to my kingdom.
Every door in my heart they open,
to let your love rush in.

I love you, is what I say when I'm talking to you.
Those words will not stay behind my lips,
because to me you are Gods gift.

My heart cries, I love you baby.
So do I, my soul chimes in.
Talking to you is a dream come true.
Loving you is as easy as eating pie.
I love you, is what I will always say,
when I find myself blessed, to be talking to you.

The Love Poem

My darling dear, have no fear, for my love is here.
My love cares not about yesterdays gone by.
My love cares only about you and I.
My love is sound and sure, because from my heart, it flows.

Your smile, your smile baby makes my heart dance.
Your eyes hypnotize me with love and affection.
Your hands were made for holding
and your lips were made for kissing.

If I could, I would grant you a thousand wishes,
so that you may obtain your hearts desires.
And I also would be wishing, that I would be
the answer, to each one of your thousand wishes.

With every breath that I take, I love you.
With every thought that I think, I love you.
With every beat of my heart, I love you.
With every feeling that I feel, I love you.

Each and everyday our love will show us the way.
Each and everyday our hearts will come together, to live and
to love.
Each and everyday we will see that the love that we've
uncovered only comes to those
who are blessed beyond measure.

My love for you, even after being pressed and shaken down
still over flow its container.
From my heart it runs like water, looking and searching for
the perfect place to go.

When I think about you and the way that I love you.
I wonder, how can this be, the strength and depth
of this love, between you and me.
It's as though we've always walked in the skies,
holding hands as we looked into each others eyes,
never to say goodbye.

If I can love you endlessly through out time, thats what I
want to do.
If I can love you when all other love in this world is gone,
thats what I intend to do.
If I can love you with the greatest love ever known to exist,
between a woman and a man, that, is my life long plan.

This Lovers Prayer

Dear Father.
You are the beginning and the end, you hold all things
in the palm of your hands.
You make the rain to fall and the waters to flow.
You make the clouds to move and the winds to blow.

Because you are father to all,
it is to you that I call.
My heart has been taken by the love of my life.
Father to you I pray and say, let not another steal her love
away.

My heart beats only because her's does. Father please, keep
us is this beautiful and real love.
Let our hearts be forever more locked in this love that
always gives, the full measure of it's self.

When lovers find a real and true love in their time,
why would they not pray?
Asking you father to let their love grow day by day.
Why would they not pray that their hearts become as one.
Why would they not pray that their undying love never
goes away.

Father please hear this prayer because our hearts are joined
together in your hands.
Father, these hearts to us you gave, they beat one with the
other.

They care the same, they honor and cherish the same.
Their love of love is identical.
The feelings these two hearts feel cannot be discerned
one from the other.

We come to you as two and not as one.
So father we pray that in this love we will always stay.
We pray and ask thee that we always treasure, honor
and cherish, this love that you sent our way.

To Finally Find Love

For some things we search high and we search low.
We search in the middle places too.
Sometimes we find a facsimile of that thing that we want to be true.
Time tells no tales, that which is good and true will always be there for you.

Once in my life time I thought that I had found a love that was true, but it turned out to be a facsimile too.
After that I felt that it really didn't matter whether I love the one I was with or not.
I found that it was easy to settle for something when the love that you loved is gone.

It's ironic that the one that I settled for, turned out to be a facsimile too.
No wonder there's a song about looking for love in all the wrong places.
As time passed, for me that which was true, stood above that which was not.
To reach the point of knowledge, wisdom and truth takes a while, in our life time.

Then one day I was messing around on the net and saw your face.
For some strange reason I was compelled to reach out to you and ask if we could just be friends and talk every now and then.
Your reply was yes, I think I would like that.

So we started to talk and laugh and smile.
But somewhere during our conversations we found
what we both had been searching for.
We looked deeply at each other thinking, that maybe this
was just a ruse.

Both of us, with tattered and bruised hearts, dared to step a
little closer.
As our hearts together began to mend we found that love
was knocking at the door, so we both opened it and our love
walked in.
Still a little shy and unsure we approached each other very
cautiously.

As we talked both of hearts continued to mend,
all of our bruises and heart aches begin to fade away.
The words that we said made our hearts and their contents
very easy to see, and we thought to ourselves, could it be,
that finally, my real and true love has come a round.

And then It seemed like out of the blue, you said
I think I've fallen in love with you. Even before that moment,
I already knew, that I had fallen in love with you.
On this journey of love we have embarked,
and now we can say, finally, finally, I have found
a love for me, that is true.

To See You For The Very First Time

When my eyes see you for the very first time,
they will record the beauty of you in my minds annals of time.
To forever be with me now and for all times.
To see again that first glimpse of you, all I have to do is think, of your loveliness.

The first touch of your hand will make me the worlds happiest man.
To see and to look into those beautiful eyes, will make me want to cry.
Cry for the love, cry for the joy and happiness, cry for all the others who do not possess a love like this.

The very first time that I taste the nectar of your lips,
we will be in another world where there is just you and just me.
There no other can exist, they will all just be shadowy images that we don't care to see.

To be with you for the very first time, for me, will be heavenly.
I can hear me calling your name, ever so softly
and I can hear you calling my name, ever so softly
as we are locked in loves embrace, for all of time.

I know that which is in your heart, your mind and your soul.
Your words are formed by these three and your words make it easy to see the things that lie within each one of these.
I also know that which is in your love.

Your love holds for you the healing of past sorrows,
it also holds the hope of a bright new tomorrow.
Your love holds for me, the key to each and everyone of my dreams.
Of your love, ballads should be written.
Of your love, stories should be told.

I know within my heart that to be loved by you is to be truly loved.
As my heart is, so is your heart, it knows no other way
but to love, when it loves, with all of its might
and to always hold precious that person who is the love of our life.

When I see you for the very first time, I will be able to touch you, to feel you, to rub you, to kiss and to hug you, all for the very first time. I will also be able to give to you for the very first time, all of my love and passion that has forever belonged to you.

To The Woman That I Love

When I think of you my heart beats full and true because in
it I can feel the love of you.
When I feel the love that I have for you
my whole world becomes real.

My body and my entire soul, your love they crave.
This love that I have inside for you
is the one thing that holds me together while we are apart.
This love that I have for you runs so deep
that at times it makes me want to weep.

I want to love you forever without end.
I want to kiss away all of your pain and sorrow.
I want you to lay your head on my shoulder
and snuggle up ever so close me.

My love I will give to you untarnished, whole and true.
Because of my love for you,
I will always want to kiss your lips, ever so long and
tenderly.
My love for you is so strong that every inch of me it has
consumed.

Do you know what I'm saying baby?
Without you, there would be no me.
Without you, there would be no us.
Without you, my life would be,
just another day spent, on the dark side of this world.

The love that I have for you baby,
there is so much inside of me that my heart just can't contain it.
And my heart lets me know everyday, thats still so.
Now I know how it feels, to be filled up, in love with you.

This love, these feelings and the care that I have for you are like being on the pinnacle of this world.

My love for you knows no day or night,
it knows no sunshine or rain,
it knows not the wind or the fire.
My love for you only knows that it's true.
My love for you only knows that where ever you are, it goes too.

Today

Today I felt lost and alone.
Because my baby's words were out of my reach.
My heart was wounded and bleeding, because
my words she could not hear.

Her love runs through my veins as life giving blood.
The mere thought of being without her sends my world
spinning out of control.
But then when I reached her again, she's there holding on
to me.
And that's when my heart sighed and said, love is love is love.

No matter the age, the shape, the size or color, love is love,
love is love.
You control all that is me, you are that which my eyes care
to see.
My lips, my lips long to press so ever softly against yours,
my eyes long only to see you.

My arms dream of surrounding you and not letting you go,
for a long, long while.
My heart jumps with anticipation of your heart being near.
My mind, my mind since you have appeared,
has never been really clear.

Your love is like the mighty storm clouds that roll through,
nothing stands in their way,
they can't be stopped by the hand of man.
To God they will only give way.

Understanding

To understand someone is to see clearly the meaning
of the words they say.
To understand someone is to know their feelings as well as
you know your own.

To know when and why a person feels a certain way
is to understand them.
Understanding is a complicated thing
because we all tend to change.

To understand is to know what's in the heart
and why it feels joy and pain.
To understand is to see, that which lies
on the inside.

I understand my woman as she understands me.
I understand my woman's heart and she understands mine.
I can tell when her heart hurts for love or pain.
She feels exactly what I feel, so our hearts feels the same.

To understand the person that you say you love,
you must first understand your self.
Understanding is not to look from the outside in,
but instead, to look from the inside out.

To be able to see through the eyes of another,
you only need to observe.
Their opinions, feelings on any topic
and their actions in there life.
To know these things of a person is to understand them.

Love requires more understanding then most other emotions
or feelings.
Love with all of it's complexities is really a very simple thing.
In this world love is not a requirement, to that man has seen.
But love is a choice bestowed upon both woman and man.

The most important understanding of all is to understand
why there is love.
To understand love, you must know love, to know love is to
give love and be willing to receive love.

Why is there Love?
If you look and listen, it's not hard to see,
that love was born in the heart of God.

Walking Toward Your Love

Toward your love is the way that I choose to go.
With each step that I make, closer am I, to your love.
Toward your love my heart beats.
Toward your love my hands reach
and toward your love my eyes always look.

Closer and closer, I have to keep walking, toward your love.
Never will I be tired or weary, from walking toward your love.
My heart moves closer, step after step, closer to your love.
My thoughts, as I walk, are filled with every thing about you.

The path that I must walk has been laid out before me,
to your love it leads, as it guides me, step by step.
It is my desire for you to know that I will never stop
walking, toward your love.

Many roads have I walked during my life time,
but till now, I had never walked, the road that leads to
your love.
My destination at the end of this road
is nothing less, than love supreme.

On this road that I walk toward your love,
my feet refuse to stop stepping.
My arms refuse to stop swinging
and my mind refuses to even consider, another path.

The condition of this road that I walk is of no consequence
because over it, my soul floats.
When I think of your love, my steps grow faster and faster.
I can feel the beating of my heart, letting me know, that I'm
walking, toward your love.

I think to myself, how can it be, someone so lovely with a
heart so pure.
Then I realize, why, this road I'm walking.
On this road there are no signs, no mile markers or
directions and for me there are no exists.

This road that I walk toward your love
is totally one way and no U-turns are allowed.
I can't truthfully say that I always walk this road toward
your love.
Because God in heaven knows, that sometimes I run.

We are Perfectly Perfect and I Wouldn't Change a Thing

A love that is perfect can only exist when there are
two hearts so intricately intertwined they beat perfectly in time.
When love is perfect, from it happiness flows, to live in
the light of a love so true makes this life perfect for me and you.

We both share a love that will never die.
We both share a love that heals our pain.
We both feel the joy of a love so tender, that if
there's distance between us, our hearts tremble.

The world has heard of but has never seen such a love
between a King and his Queen.
A love that is so perfectly perfect that people stop and stare
because a love that perfect inundates the air.

A perfect heart can only see through perfect eyes.
Perfect words can only be uttered through perfect lips.
A perfect smile can only appear on a perfect face.
A perfect love can only join together two perfect hearts.

Let us cry from the mountain tops,
"We are Perfectly Perfect" as our love is perfectly perfect.
The very centers of our essence holds and clings to each other
and there is no place left for anything that is not perfectly perfect.

As the sun and the moon are perfectly perfect so that we may live,
so is the love that fills our hearts and it, to each other we give.
Our love grows, it seem by leaps and bounds, just because we know each others perfect sound.

We were made by perfect hands, the same that made man to live and stand.
Those same hands spread forth mercy and love.
By the hands of God we were made, from sand, clay and mud.
Because God made us in his image our love is made in the image of his love, therefore,
"We are Perfectly Perfect and I Wouldn't Change a Thing."

Dedecated to
"MY Ruky Love"
Rukayatu Suleiman Irons

What Can I Say About Love

As a man that was given a heart that loves deeper than any
other heart and with that same heart feels feelings
stronger than others ever could.
As that man, what can I tell you about love?

The first thing that I would tell you is that love feels good
and that it hurts.
Love can work miracles but it can also let you down.
Love is like holding on to something extra tight.
Love is like begging, baby, baby please!

You can't hide from love because it already knows your name.
Love seems to come most unexpectedly.
Love is for the heart like the air that we breath.
Love is blind and maybe that's why it doesn't care about time.

What else can the guy with the tender heart tell you about
love?
I can tell you that it can come and go
and I can also tell you that it can come and stay.
I can tell you that if you are really bitten by the love bug, it's
there to the end.

Being in love is like the night side of day,
you're alway searching to find your way.
Love can make you or break you, it's just that simple.
Love can also heal all the hearts that need mending.

What else should I tell you about love?
Love is like a fortress sitting high on a hill,
it must be protected at all costs.

Love is like the air that we breath,
it also nourishes the heart, mind, body and soul.

Love is like a food that everybody needs.
Love can quench the thirst of loneliness and sorrow.
Love can guide you in the way that you should go.
Love will hide nothing from you, it's always there for you to see.

The last things that I will tell you about love, are these,
Walk with love, each step that you take.
Then you will be able to run with love, into heavens gates.

What Is It

What is it about you that makes me want to call your name in the middle of the night?
What is it about you that makes me want to hold you and hold you all through the night?
What is it about you that makes me lose my emotional self control?
What is it about you that makes me want to love and to have you, through all of time?

What is it in your smile that makes my heart skip a beat?
What is it in the sound of your voice thats so tantalizing to me?
What is it in your eyes that I see, that simply lift me off my feet?
What is it with this desire that I have, to put a ring on that finger and make you mine for all of time?

What is it about you that has my heart under your complete control?
What is it about your love that makes it so hot, that I don't ever want it to stop?
What is it about your beauty that runs so deep and true, that makes me barely able to stand, being away from you?

What is it that you do to keep me loving and loving you?
What is it in your words of love that humble my soul?
What is it in your heart that make my heart rejoice?
What is it in your love that makes my love forever, want to be in your heart?

What is it in you that makes me crave the taste of your lips?
What is it in you that makes me worry about how I should hold your hand?
What is about you, that makes me smile and stare, at every picture I see of you?
What is it, what is it, that makes me do the things that I do for you?

What is it, that something, that thing?
It's all about you baby,
it's your warm and tender love, that to me, you have given.

A man I would not be, if I didn't treasure your love tremendously.
A man I would not be, If I failed to love you with all the love that is within me.
Neither would I be a man if I ever failed, to hold your loving hand.

As I have always been, I will always be your man.
I am the man who loves you just the way you are.
I am the man who will forever, caress, kiss and hug you.
I am the man whose heart you have stolen.
And I am the man whose heart, is yours to forever hold.

When I Knew That I Loved You

My heart had been torn between something I was already
trying to do and something in my life that was new.
I will never forget that night how your voice
just went all through me.

You called my name and you said.
Just come get me! Just come get me!

At that moment my heart was no longer torn
between two things because then I realized
that the most important thing was right there in front of me.

That's when I knew that I had to do what ever I needed to do,
to spend the rest of my life with you.
At that moment, in a way, we stood face to face,
looking at each other to see what we could see.

You were not looking at the outer man
and I was not looking at the outer woman.
We both were looking into each others hearts
as deep as we could see, looking for the love
that had so long eluded, both you and me.

When I looked into your heart that night
I found that illusive love and the woman of my dreams.
Just as I had given up on finding a love that was worth
having, in the split of a second, there you were, like a flash
of lighting.

Then I knew that my heart had been captivated by you.
From that night on my love for you was out of my control.
Til this day I still think and wonder, how can a man
be so blessed to have your love come his way.

Right now as I speak to you my heart feels full and it feels empty.
My heart is full of our love and your love and my love for you.
But because love is love the way it is, it must be fulfilled.
There's an empty spot in my heart because we are apart
thats waiting for you, to be filled.

Where Do You Start

When you want to tell someone just how much you care, searching for words to say and when you find them the question is, where do you start?

Do you start by telling her that just by knowing her, your life is but a dream.
Do you start by saying, you are my every waking thought.
Do you start by telling her that, her inner beauty causes the winds to blow.
Do you start by just simply saying, I would die for you.

All the things that I think and all the things that I say evolves around your love.
I see you constantly in the eyes of my mind, you are always there, I need only but to look and see.
Every step into the tomorrow brings us that much closer to where we want and need to be.

Step by step, come and walk with me.
Dance with me in the heavens amongst the stars and may we twinkle just as bright as they are.
Come and glide with me along the moon beams that shine form sea to sea.
Come and talk with me as through the skies of heaven we sail.

You are the tick in my tick tock as each second passes by.
You are like the ringing of church bells that say, come, let us pray.

Warmth and love exudes from you like the water of a fountain.
Your heart is pure, your love is true, you are the hope of a great love.
You are the faith that makes the world stand as a good place for all of man.

In the depths of my heart a deep, strong and burning love lives.
This love is like no other.
This love hurts with a soothing pain.
This love excites and arouses.
This love is that for which I will fight.
This love holds my heart so tight!
This love is my minds delight .
This love through God is right.

Where there is great love such as yours,
there is greater compassion, greater sympathy,
a greater sense of caring and a greater need to share that love.

I am here to share of your love as you share of mine.
Timeless and endless is the love that I will give to you.
I will start by just saying, I love you.

Why Do I Love You So

Is it because you give all of you to me.
Or is it because I give all of me to you.
I only know that when you give love it returns many fold.

The heart controls who we love
and where our love goes.
Why do I love you so?
The answer to that question only my heart knows.

Maybe I love you so because of that look
that's in your eyes.
Or perhaps it's the smile that adorns your sweet, sweet lips.
To me you are the personification of love it self.

I asked myself why do I love you so.
After thinking a moment, myself replied, because she's your
hearts gold, because she completes your soul.

To love anyone as deeply as I love you, for me, is to be in
unexplored territory.
There in my life I have never been.
The sweetness of you knows no kin.

Why do I love you so,
maybe it's because you never let my love go.
My love is for your love
and your love is for my love.

Why do I love you so,
is it because my heart tells me day by day
that your love is the only way for me to go.
Or is it because my heart will feel for no other.

I love you so my baby, because you are all that I need.
I love you so my darling because my heart has given
its self to you down on bended knees.
I love you so my love because you are my love,
my heart and my soul.

Why Does love Hurt

Love is not something that you can put in your hands and
then run away.
True love cannot be bought or sold, it must be found and
then received.
Love is the greatest of all gifts, It will warm, feed and
nourish you.
But because love is so strong and powerful, sometimes, it
tends to hurt.

Loves home is the heart, one of the most finicky of things.
The heart controls the flow of love, in and out.
The heart can let love die or it can give it sustaining life.
The heart and love often battle it out,
maybe thats another reason why, sometimes, love hurts.

Contrary to some's popular belief,
love cannot be owned, just freely given.
Love is kissing your sweetheart and never wanting to let go,
but you must in order to live.
There again is when, sometimes, love hurts.

Love can make you smile, laugh and cry, all in the blink of
an eye.
Love can give you the happiness of the whole world it
seems.
True love is very hard to find and so easy to lose.
When you have searched and finally found the one
love that was meant for you, love in that case
can also hurt, so good.

One would think that the heart and love walk hand and hand,
but they are two different entities.
The hearts main purpose is to give life but it also feels love,
love it needs to receive and love it needs to give.

Love is a force to be reckoned with.
Love is the greatest power known to man,
but yet, is man to really hold it in his hands.
Love can heal the wounds of the world
if we only wanted it to, and sometimes, thats why love hurts.

The love between a man and a woman is the truest example of
God's love that we have and can see. If that love is real,
it can be as strong as God's love for us all.
A love that only knows a beginning.
Love hurts because, sometimes, it has to.

Your Sensuality

Your sensuality cannot be denied, it only takes one look into your eyes.
To be sensual is to entice with overwhelming beauty.
To be sensual is to speak in tones so soft but yet so deep that the sound stirs my soul, my mind and heart you control.

When a woman is sensual she has a natural flare for the intimate and personal things she wants to share.
Her eyes tell the stories of untold love.
Her movements and posture all blend together creating loves dare.

Everything about her says the likes of me you have never seen.
She can move all who see her with her sensuality.
With just one look or just a glancing glow shock waves of passion begin flow.

Your sultry demeanor incapacitates.
You move with the smoothest sensual glide that pulls feeling from deep down inside.
No eyes can look away from your beauty, no not for just one second.

When your eyes turn and look at me my heart melts instantly.
When you approach and take my hand every other man sticks his head in the sand.
For what good is it to see and never hold such rare beauty.

When I think about the way you walk, the way you talk,
the way you smile and the way you laugh, I know
that sensuality has just held a class.

It is good for a woman to be attractive or pretty.
But for a woman to possess such astounding beauty and
then move as though she's sliding on silk
as her smile melts my heart into a thousand little pieces.
Your sensuality truly captivates me.

I am a prisoner of her love. Please, no pardon do I want.
Just give me life without the possibility of parole.

CPSIA information can be obtained
at www.ICGtesting.com
Printed in the USA
BVHW04s2302221018
530937BV00009B/154/P